IT'S TIME TO EAT YAMS

It's Time to Eat YAMS

Walter the Educator

Silent King Books
A WhichHead Entertainment Imprint

Copyright © 2024 by Walter the Educator

All rights reserved. No part of this book may be reproduced in any manner whatsoever without written per- mission except in the case of brief quotations embodied in critical articles and reviews.

First Printing, 2024

Disclaimer

This book is a literary work; the story is not about specific persons, locations, situations, and/or circumstances unless mentioned in a historical context. Any resemblance to real persons, locations, situations, and/or circumstances is coincidental. This book is for entertainment and informational purposes only. The author and publisher offer this information without warranties expressed or implied. No matter the grounds, neither the author nor the publisher will be accountable for any losses, injuries, or other damages caused by the reader's use of this book. The use of this book acknowledges an understanding and acceptance of this disclaimer.

It's Time to Eat YAMS is a collectible early learning book by Walter the Educator suitable for all ages belonging to Walter the Educator's Time to Eat Book Series. Collect more books at WaltertheEducator.com

USE THE EXTRA SPACE TO TAKE NOTES AND DOCUMENT YOUR MEMORIES

YAMS

It's time to eat, the yams are here,

It's Time to Eat

Yams

Soft and sweet, they bring us cheer.

Orange and warm, they shine so bright,

Yams are ready, take a bite!

Grown in the soil, deep and snug,

Yams are like treasure under the rug.

Farmers dig them up with care,

Now they're waiting to share and share.

Bake them up, or mash them down,

Yams can wear a golden brown crown.

Add a sprinkle of spice or a little sweet,

Every yam is a tasty treat.

Roast them slow or fry them fast,

Yams are the food that always lasts.

With cinnamon sprinkles or marshmallow fluff,

Just one bite is never enough.

It's Time to Eat

Yams

Cut them in cubes or make a pie,

Yams are magic, we can't deny.

Creamy and smooth or crispy delight,

Yams are perfect day or night.

They give us energy, help us grow,

Yams are healthy, and that we know.

For running and jumping and having fun,

Yams are food for everyone.

In soups or stews or all alone,

Yams are a food we're glad to own.

On the table, they sit with pride,

A yummy joy we won't let slide.

Pass the yams and take a turn,

For their goodness, we'll always yearn.

Warm and cozy, soft as can be,

It's Time to Eat

Yams

Yams are perfect for you and me.

Let's thank the yams for all they do,

Helping us grow strong and true.

It's time to eat, let's dig right in,

Yams make us smile again and again!

Now cheer for yams, let's all agree,

They're the best, as sweet as can be.

Clap your hands, do a little dance,

It's Time to Eat

Yams

Yams are love at every chance!

ABOUT THE CREATOR

Walter the Educator is one of the pseudonyms for Walter Anderson. Formally educated in Chemistry, Business, and Education, he is an educator, an author, a diverse entrepreneur, and he is the son of a disabled war veteran. "Walter the Educator" shares his time between educating and creating. He holds interests and owns several creative projects that entertain, enlighten, enhance, and educate, hoping to inspire and motivate you. Follow, find new works, and stay up to date with Walter the Educator™ at WaltertheEducator.com

Milton Keynes UK
Ingram Content Group UK Ltd.
UKHW010227111224
452348UK00011B/555